Prince Pounce-a-Lot

By

Fay Lorraine Sueltz

AuthorHouse™
1663 Liberty Drive
Bloomington, IN 47403
www.authorhouse.com
Phone: 1 (800) 839-8640

© 2015 Fay Lorraine Sueltz. All rights reserved.

Story, images and photography by Fay Lorraine Sueltz

No part of this book may be reproduced, stored in a retrieval system, or transmitted by any means without the written permission of the author.

Published by AuthorHouse 09/09/2016

ISBN: 978-1-5049-5549-2 (sc)
ISBN: 978-1-5049-5857-8 (e)

Library of Congress Control Number: 2015918710

Print information available on the last page.

Any people depicted in stock imagery provided by Thinkstock are models, and such images are being used for illustrative purposes only. Certain stock imagery © Thinkstock.

This book is printed on acid-free paper.

Because of the dynamic nature of the Internet, any web addresses or links contained in this book may have changed since publication and may no longer be valid. The views expressed in this work are solely those of the author and do not necessarily reflect the views of the publisher, and the publisher hereby disclaims any responsibility for them.

authorHOUSE®

Dedicated to
My Dolly
From Prince

The book captures Prince's real life adventures.
The Post Script contains information about the amazing
abilities of dogs in their service to humans.

Special Thanks to:

*Mary Batchelder, Robin MacFadden Parrish, James Hudgens, Sandra Gustafson,
and David Coddon's UCSD Creative Writing Class
for preliminary reading and comments.*

And

*Tracey Lombardi, Barbie Thompson, Susan Fox, the Pet Therapy Volunteers and Staff at
Scripps Memorial Hospital and Prince Pounce-a-Lot for encouragement and support,*

Fay Lorraine

Preface

While out for a summer evening walk along the outdoor cafes in Coronado, California, I noticed a delightful and elegant black and white fluffy dog sitting tall beside a dinner table. She was gorgeous! Not knowing what to expect, I asked her owner about the breed of the striking animal. "Standard Poodle" was the reply and I was invited to pet her. Her name was Dolly and her gentle nature and soft curls had me asking more questions. I had no idea poodles came in the size of a Labrador retriever, only much taller.

Dolly's breeder had several pups available for adoption at the time I met her and I was given the contact information.

When I called to discuss owning a Standard Poodle with Dolly's dog breeder, I was assured that my apartment with only a balcony to the outdoors would be a fine home for a poodle puppy. Poodles, I was told, like to be in close contact with their humans. When not racing around outdoors under supervision, they become couch potatoes near their owner's feet.

I went to just take a look at the breeder's puppies a few days later. Once there, I fell for my Prince.

In further research on my own later, I discovered the Poodle's original size as a hunting dog is about 40-60 lbs. "Pudlehoud" in German, or "puddle hound dog" in English, was the name first given to a breed of these hunting dogs developed in Germany sometime at the end of the 1700's. As part of a hunting team, these curly haired water dogs were trained to flush fowl by pouncing in watery marshes, directing the bird's flight in front of their human counterparts. Fowl downed by the hunter's guns were then retrieved by the dogs from lakes and marshlands and brought to their human hunting partners. The name of the breed was shortened to just "pudle" or as we now say "poodle".

In France, these German hunting dogs were bred into a miniature size and made the national dog of France, the French Poodle. The American Kennel club recognizes poodles in three sizes: Standard, Miniature and Toy. Because of their amazing learning abilities, poodles have assumed a wide variety of occupations besides hunting. Wonderful family and companion dogs, they pull sleds for their masters in Alaska, are able to herd about 100 sheep at a time and make exceptional Service Dogs, guiding the blind and assisting other disabled people with various tasks.

Prince's problem solving abilities and raw emotional intelligence are of constant amazement to me. He understands many words. He quickly sizes people and dogs up as "ok" to approach, ignore or to completely avoid.

Just today at a local dog park, he stopped playing with his ball and stood with ears cocked and tail parallel to the ground in his "alert" stance. I followed his gaze to see a pet timber wolf playing with three other dogs. Giving the animal wide birth, his curiosity failed him. Prince moved backwards towards the gate and closer to me at the same time, asking to leave the park. We left and he and the wolf smelled each other's noses through the wire fence as we passed quickly on our way home. A polite "hello" through the fence was close enough for Prince on that adventure!

He understands pain in others. As an example, while still a very independent pup, Prince loved to play a fast running circle game around me. He would start the game by innocently asking to go to the end of the leash to sniff a flower or tree, and then just take off like a little wild bull. Pulling at random intervals hard against the leash, he knocked me off balance. I braced myself while twirling around with him, pulling that smiling dog to me hand over hand. Once he got the game going, it was difficult to stop him. He enjoyed directing my actions. My calling out for him to "sit, sit and stay!" was the music he enjoyed while dancing with me as his captive partner.

The last time he did this little running dance, the leash caught on my fourth right hand finger as I struggled to move fast enough to keep up with his circling. On one of his random jerks of the leash I felt my finger tearing painfully in my hand. Without words, I swallowed hard as we looked into each other's eyes. He put his head down, and slowly approached. Looking at me, looking away, tail wagging slowly, he licked the broken part of my hand. How did he know my hand was hurting? He never played his circle game again.

I will continue in the Post Script about our relationship from my point of view. The Post Script will also contain documented scientific information about the amazing abilities of dogs in their service to humans. Now however, I let Prince use his own words about our life together.

Here is his story:

My First Home

My first memories are of the warmth and comfort of my mother, Britte. A favorite poodle at our breeding house, she was the smallest of the sixteen adult dogs living there at that time. Often invited to jump to the master's lap to rest or take a short nap, Britte was a clever and very sweet Standard Poodle.

As one of her eight new June babies I joined in the constant jostling around her in our happy puppy pen. We pups tested the sturdiness of our new bodies against each other in clumsy games of roll-together "tag" and mock battle.

In preparation for our future of living with people, Britte told us we must always be loving and warm to visitors. We must never bite down hard or ever scratch anyone. We watched her every move, well, when we weren't playing, which was, ok - most of the time!

Sometimes when we were busy eating or playing close to her, Britte would sing this little tune to us, "Be loving and awesome - and - you will be chosen - by a nice person!"

"Away from you Mom?" I asked her, and I thought oh no! I wanted to stay and play and learn from her for a long time.

Britte smiled and said, "You will see. Life will be good!"

A nuzzle from Mom under the chin reinforced our good behavior and a gruff grab at the back of our neck scolded us. Out of all the songs she sang to us, my favorite one still comes to mind, "Keep your cool as long as doggedly doable… whenever you find it possible." She would sing this softly whenever she spread herself out on cool tile or shaded grass, inviting us to join her.

Even now as a grown dog, I hardly pass cool long grass without asking to lie down and roll over a few times in it. The coolness, the smell, and the taste of long grass brings me back to easy times of resting in the big shaded lawn of my first home. As I roll over and over, I sing my family songs, which probably sound like strange moaning to most people around. I beat my tail with pleasure in time to my tunes, refreshed by happy puppy memories.

Who's Next?

Several other play pens in our breeder's house were filled with pups of different ages. Their mothers stayed with them, teaching them constantly. When we grew larger, we all played together in a large outdoor pen.

Visiting people would come into the large pen to play with us during the day. Sometimes a visitor would take a pup away with them when they left, not to return. This didn't seem to bother the grown dogs or the people at our house. Who would be next? It was the talk of the puppy pen.

It was in this outdoor pen filled with toys and things to climb upon that I met a lively black and white pup. She and I fell in together as friends immediately. She taught me hide – and – seek, and how to politely ask for treats from visitors to our pen. I remember how she would run around the pen to find me. She always sniffed inside my ear, to make sure it was me! Bowing low, she made a show of inviting me to play with her in front of everyone. We each waited for the perfect chance to surprise – dive in to the other, laughing and rolling together. She called me a "real rascal". Her important lessons in how to have fun have served me all my life and I was her willing student.

A visitor with long brown hair often came into the large outdoor pen. This lady always brought fun with her to share with us and she had never taken a pup away.

Busy playing with my best friend, I didn't pay too much attention to the brown – haired lady when she arrived one afternoon. I scooted into a nice hiding place behind some flower pots. I held my breath. When my friend didn't find me right away I yipped, "Puppy! Puppy, I'm over here, come and find me!" There was no answer.

Finally I peeked between the flowers. Surprise! My good friend sat on the lap of the lady visitor, calmly nosing the lady's arm. The lady held her close, talking to her and laughing. Then the lady stood up and opened the gate of the play pen. But she didn't put my friend back in the pen. She was still holding the black and white pup as she closed the gate and walked away! My best puppy friend had been chosen as the next pup to leave! I ran yelping to my Mom and found her standing beside my friend's mother. They sniffed the air and smiled as the pup got in a car with the visitor. Turning to me Britte said, "Did you see how your friend ran right up to the lady?" She exhaled, beaming with pride.

"Naw…I was in the flowers."

"In the flowers?"

"Yeah, we were playing, and she was 'it', so I hid in the flowers," I said in a hollow voice. "I didn't see them get together at all." The car put a dusty distance between me and my good friend.

"Well, I saw them, and they both seem quite happy." Britte's words seemed solid and round. "Come little pup, let's -"

I started to tremble and sniffed back a big tear. "Oh Mom, if I hadn't been behind the flowers, she would still be here!" How could I have let her go away?

"Little pup, let's go out to the grass and talk," Britte spoke softly as she lowered her tail and led the way to a tree shaded spot. We both flopped down. Her eyes moistened as motherly joy gave way to serious talk.

"Sweet little man, all puppies are chosen sooner or later, playing or not, hiding or not hiding, it does not matter," Britte's voice soothed me. At the same time the meaning of her words made me uncomfortable.

"Your fluffy friend is with very good person," she spoke calmly.

"Oh Mom," I whispered, licking a long stray blade of grass into my mouth tasting its summer sweetness. I guessed my friend was as lucky as any of us pups were going to be. Why did we have to leave home?

"Think about her having a wonderful new life. Think of her happiness." my Mom continued, "Try not to think about 'You'."

"Yeah Mom…," I exhaled all my air into a small voice, blowing the grass blade to the ground. But I wasn't thinking of "Me", I was just *feeling* sad. I tilted my body and rested on my side with my legs stretched straight out, and my head close to Mom.

"These people seem strong and able to do many things," she continued. "They give us food and water. They bathe us and they give us comfortable places to play and rest, all things that would be hard for us to find in their world without them. Yet, some of them know they need our help and not just our friendship in this, their world. Be polite and loving to the visitors and get ready for a life of adventure with one of them. Let your person be your Top Dog. Do you understand? Your friend is just starting her adventure now."

She began to sing one of our family songs, low and soothing. I licked her paw and put my nose deep into the grass. "Puppy, let me smell you, give you a cuddle?" Britte asked in a voice just a whisper above the sound of the soft summer breeze that surrounded my sorrow. Feeling too sad and lazy to rise up, I dug my toenails into the sod pulling my small body close enough to receive Mom's welcome nuzzle under my muzzle.

I thought, good speech Mom, but why not invite a visitor to stay there with our pack? Why should I leave my Mom? I didn't tell Britte, but I began to give my favorite visitors little puppy nips. I was saying, "I like you! Stay with me and join our dog pack here!"

Her Name is Dolly!

My brothers and sisters were chosen, one, two, and three, they left with visitors. I continued to greet the people I liked with friendly nips, "Hello! Please stay here!" Then soon, four, five, and six of Britte's pups were chosen and taken away. I played with newer, younger pups in the big pen. Once in a while my favorite black and white puppy friend would visit us with her new lady. She always sought me out for a little rough house play whenever she came, which made us both happy. Dolly was her name. She was the center of attention at her new home and her lady was very good to her. "My lady cooks for me. Rabbit, I love eating rabbit!" I was truly happy for her and listening to her stories made me *almost* want to have my own person and new life too. Almost….

Freedom for my Dolly!

Sitting calmly next to her lady, Dolly was already in the outdoor pen when I arrived one afternoon to play with all the pups. Bowing my head low to her, I wagged my entire puppy body, inviting her to play.

"Not now little guy, see?" My best friend whispered. With her habit of not moving her head at all, she rolled her eyes from looking straight ahead at me to fixing her gaze on her leash, which was down low and almost behind her. Her ability to rotate her eyes far and wide within their sockets always amazed me. "I am tied to my lady's chair. I can't move too far today, sorry," she continued. "Let's just talk quietly right here."

"Oh…no problem, I won't talk at all…grrrumph." I quietly settled into chewing through her pretty pink leash. Soon my friend was free to play! I had my way of making things happen, for sure!

"My smart little Rascal." Dolly bowed, "Let's play!" Her long fluffy tail waved like a flag.

"What? My name is 'Puppy', not 'Rascal'." I bounced away from her, lifting my chin to look tall and regal on my stubby fluffy legs. I was secretly so wild inside with the idea that she thought I was smart!

"Everyone's name is 'Puppy' at our house. You were 'Puppy' too, remember, before you were 'Dolly'?"

"When you get a person, you will get a name too." Dolly waved her tail for emphasis. Bouncing back to her, I guessed she would think me to be the smartest puppy that ever lived when I told her about my nipping plan. But Dolly just laughed. She was always fun to be around because even the smallest amusement gave her great joy which spilled over into everyone around her.

"You think someone will want you because you BITE them?" She laughed so hard she had to sit and then lie completely down. "AND, not only *that*, but you think that person will want to stay here in a puppy pen with you and your Mom? Ha ha ha! If and when you finally get a person, that person will name you too, you teeny wild pup! Although I'm naming you Rascal, because you really are one!" She shook with giggles.

Dolly rolled onto her back and continued a low howling laugh, her four feet waving in the air, the long fur of her tail sweeping the floor, "You better love the person up who chooses you, you little smart guy. You think too much maybe, Rascal? Ha ha."

"Ha ha ha yourself." I yelped back, but her laughter made me laugh too. My mouth turned into a huge smile, showing most of my teeny baby teeth. I pounced on her belly and we rolled together laughing for a long time – until her lady took her home. Her visits never came soon enough for me.

My Day Arrives At Long Last

Well, at least my nipping plan was good enough for Dolly to think and talk about. And at least according to my plan, I still lived at home. Well, it was my home wasn't it? Maybe my plan would cause a person to laugh, like Dolly had laughed. It was good to be around people and dogs who laughed a lot, so I stuck to my plan.

One of my brothers and I were the only two left from our puppy litter when we were four months old. Around this time the day came that I met my person. It happened as a few of us pups played in the big pen. A lady came in and sat quietly on a bench, petting us all as we came to her. Then, after nosing up to her and leaving a couple times, I trotted directly up to the lady with serious intent to nip her, to ask her to join our pack. Why not? She seemed nice and smart enough to understand me.

As I approached, she placed her hands deep into my wooly warm fur. Then squeezing me softly along my whole body, she hugged me for a long time. I stood still and as tall as my short little legs would allow, soaking up her love. I bowed my head then nipped her leg softly – twice, then licked her arm as she stroked my fur. "I like you!" said my nip, "Join our pack here. Little doggies are going away. We need you HERE!"

She smiled and quietly said something I did not understand, yet the music of her voice called me to attention with pleasure. She understood my nipping talk, and spoke to the owner of the breeding house before leaving that day.

Two days later, she came back, smiled and lifted me up. While looking at each other face to face, all at once I understood that she was just another visitor wanting to take a pup away. This time, I was that pup! All the talk about having my own person someday had suddenly come true.

The warmth of her affection melted my nipping plan. An intense desire to reach her face was the only thing left inside of me. I kicked the air, squirming wildly to lick, lick, and wildly lick her cheek. I must have looked like a large wiggle worm of joy. The lady laughed, hugged me close saying "My Prince!" She repeated that word, Prince, as she took me away in our car. Prince was my name! I wanted to find Dolly and tell her that I had a name too.

My New Home

She seemed to answer to the name 'Lori,' so I thought of her as 'My Lady Lori.' She showed me my food and water dishes and let me wander around my new place. Everything was so new, so strange. First of all, I searched to find my family. Could they be here too?

Singing the songs I was taught as a tiny pup about being good and loving to others helped calm me. I hummed and sang my family tunes on top of each other, "… keep your cool as long as doggedly do-able…hmmm…you will get a nice person… hmmm…it's awesome… possible…hmmm." Memories of my Mom and puppy friends came with me into the new rooms where I sang my songs.

One strange thing I met that first day had pointed ears and was about my size. I met the marmalade colored fluff ball as I wandered into the food room.

"OH! Another pup!" I thought bowing low to invite the strange looking doggie to play. About the same length as his body, his long tail seemed to be a complete and separate animal.

"NOW, Me-ow!" His back bowed into an arch as he and his tail floated up to a counter top and out of my reach.

"I am David, a cat. And you are a dog, and you must leave me alone! Meow, NOW, NOW. " Lori came in to stroke his back. Relaxing as he sat beneath her hand, David licked his paw and just stared at me.

"Well, I just wanted to play." I wandered out of the room. Lori followed me. She showed me my plush new bed. For me this was the best discovery that first day. I turned two circles around it and flopped down into a deep sleep.

The next day, I discovered many new toys, including a large red rubber ball. The ball was thrown for me across the room or outdoors. I would rear up and POUNCE forcefully on it! It would fly up again, and I jumped along with it, pushing it towards the ground until it settled between my front feet. I bit at it while squeezing the yielding rubber with strong puppy toes. The ball would squish out sideways from my grasp. I would pounce on it again. Lori often called me to come to her when it was in my mouth. I would toss my head and laugh, biting hard into the rubber ball. Lori admired my pouncing game. She had little choice, as I rarely brought the ball back to her. She often had to put on my leash and pull me along saying, "Come along my sweet Prince Pounce – a – Lot, it's time to go now."

David

The apartment came with a pleasant outdoor balcony filled with plants. And David. He came before me on the feeding schedule. He talked about half the time he was awake. Much of what he said made at least a bit of sense, "Let me outside! Now! Now! Pet me!! NOW! Open the screen door to the balcony! Now, now NOW! Have a Purr Purrfect purrpurrpurrfect sleep…now…purr."

He and I didn't speak much to each other, mostly because I would pretend to be asleep when he talked, or I would actually fall asleep.

Sometimes Lori took me along when she walked David outdoors. He nibbled on fresh tall grass or other leaves of his choice. Sod clumps of his favorite plants were neatly kept in "David's garden", a small pot on the balcony, for his later snacking.

David's happy and special bond with My Lady Lori was something wonderful that I could never share or ever wish to break.

His fluffy belly flipped from side to side in rhythm with the bobbing of his head while his tail seemed to move with a personality all on its own. He was a walking – talking invitation to be chased.

No Means NO!

And chasing David is how I learned the meaning of the word "NO!" My Lady Lori never struck me or David when that cat teased me to chase him. She has never hit us at all, even to this day. However the tone of her voice shamed me in a way that only a dog can be shamed.

And to be leashed and tied to her chair was humiliating. Doing this said that she didn't trust me at all. When a person does not trust a dog, life is hard for both of them.

David's cat mind was not capable of learning about "NO!" Protected by his natural indifference to any given command, he never seemed to be humiliated, nor was he ever even humble.

David

So, it was all up to me to withstand his teasing without a chase. But I learned, against my better instinct, well, my hunting instinct anyway, to just watch him as he bobbed by me or as he jumped up to places where I could not see or even imagine where he would land.

Peacefully snoozing one afternoon, I suddenly woke to a sudden breeze that smelled like David. That cat was running by almost on top of me! His tail spanked my nose as he squeaked, "Now! Now! Bird! Bird on rail, now!" He hurried after some shadow floating along the screen door at our balcony.

Rocketing up while staying in place I yelped, "Cat, get that cat!"

"No!" Lori's face was serious.

"grrr… that cat…get cat….the tail…" I stood still whimpering,

"Good boy, my Prince!"

A great back rubbing distracted me from thinking of that tease of a cat. I turned my back on David right then and there. If I couldn't see him, I wouldn't chase him.

I pretended that he was a vision, just a dream I was seeing while awake. Turning my back on him whenever he came hopping along swaying his fluffy belly near my nose became my best effort at obedience. I guess many people could learn a trick from me - a dog. Just turn your back on things that are wrong to do and avoid them!

Patient Love

A big black box on a table seemed to be Lori's favorite toy. She sat in a chair in front of it moving her fingers to make the box show colors and change colors. The way she played with that box wasn't like the fun I knew about, the fun of pouncing on a ball.

Playing should be fun. When I thought she had too much of this toy, when she worried about the colors in front of her, I sat on her feet. Other times I licked her hand. Then she would place her hands deep into my fur. "Oh, my Prince! How about a walk right now… to Dog Beach?"

Those were tail wagging words! The mention of Dog Beach made me jump around. If calming her was to be one of my jobs, it certainly came with benefits! Shutting the colors off and laughing at my goofiness transported her into my "right now" world. Most times when we returned from our walks she finished playing with her lighted toy quickly.

Exploration and Discovery

About every day we walked to Dog Beach, Coronado. Dogs ran there without leashes. We sniffed and chased each other, and we all just splashed around in wet sandy puddles. I had never seen so much of that wet stuff, that *water,* in one place as there was at Dog Beach. Most of the other dogs ran full speed into the water, splashing and creating foaming white water. I stepped into calm water near the shore, but I ran from moving water when it curved high and made that crashing sound with white bubbles.

Prince Pounce-a-Lot
at Coronado Dog Beach

"Thank you, thank you," I would say by licking My Lady's hand. Before and after our visits to dog beach.

I liked to make fun of myself doing things, to make Lori laugh. While walking next to a wall we had passed many times, one day I quickly thought, 'Why just walk down low on the ground all the time? I can go the same way, but up on the wall, closer to Lori. Let me try it.' So up I jumped, at first walking slowly toe over toe, glancing back at Lori and smiling. She started to laugh so hard it got my tail wagging. Walking toe over toe along a skinny wall is not so easy in the first place. My tail became a rudder, safely pulling me to either side of the wall just as I would begin to slide off. I kept up my fast pace. Toe over toe, I wobbled along the wall.

Prince of Dog Beach, Coronado!

Just before I completely lost my balance, I jumped down and continued trotting along as if nothing had happened. It was as if I had never jumped up on the wall in the first place. Lori laughed even harder and I turned and smiled back at her.

The Poodle Party

Placing me into a back seat dog hammock of our car one day, My Lady repeated the word "Dolly" to me as we drove away from our home and away from Dog Beach.

"Dolly" had a fuzzy friendly meaning in my mind. I couldn't remember just what it meant. But when we parked, and I jumped from the car, far away across green grass I saw something familiar. A slender black and white shape moved between several solid colored poodles. Dolly! My good friend Dolly and I were both invited to a poodle party in the Bay Park. While dancing with several poodle pups and big poodles she called to me, "HEY! Hey, Rascal!" I heard her voice, "Rascal! You, my little Rascal." Dolly remembered me, wow! Did I run?

No.

I flew to her.

We took turns chasing each other and rolled together in a poodle pile, tossing ourselves over and over on the grass, laughing and squirming against each other.

"My Doll!" I cried, "My name is Prince!"

"Be polite and let me introduce you to everyone, little Rascal, I mean, my Princeling," Dolly composed herself circling toward the small pack of dog visitors coaxing me, "Let's all play together!" She led me to the dog pack.

"Hi guys!" I nuzzled a quick hello to the nearest pups, a few of whom I knew from my days at the breeder's home. But all they could do was stand and watch as I repeatedly teased Dolly out of the dog pack to play only with me. Even back then she was definitely *my Dolly*, and I told her so.

She made me laugh as she kept her head in the same place while rolling her big brown eyes away from the most handsome poodle at the party. She turned her gaze to take a sidelong glance at me. I was still half her size back then. I bowed my head to her.

"Me, your Doll? Ha ha, you little Rascal!" She turned to face me and bowed right in front of me, wagging her long fluffy flag tail. "Ha!" She repeated, "Come on, let's play!"

"Ha yourself! I will catch you!" I yelped with joy because she had invited only me to play in front of every poodle there! We ran round and round while she tagged me, ran and then let me catch up to her. After running so hard, I slowed down and asked for water. Resting and drinking, I licked and licked My Lady's hand in thanks for bringing me to the poodle party.

"So the Little Rascal has found a home after all." I looked up to see Ranger, the big handsome poodle, striking up a conversation with Dolly.

Cocking my head to one side, I charged Ranger while gathering a crowd of pups close behind me. Everyone there seemed to expect a fight between Ranger and me. But my clever Dolly pivoted quickly away from Ranger and toward me asking softly, "So, Prince – Rascal, how is it going for you now in your new place?" Her steady voice calmed me and I pounced to a halt beside her, my ear at her elbow.

After a few deep breaths I told the crowd about my kind treatment, my wonderful ball, my crazy new brother David, and all about our visits to Dog Beach.

"Wow! You hit the beach almost every day?" Truly impressed, Ranger stepped away from Dolly and me as he continued, "I love to leap into shallow white water, land on a wave, and let it lift me from the ground. I feel like a birdie, it seems like flying for a few moments!" Ranger sighed and smiled at me.

"You lucky pup, flying all the time!" A younger pup spoke softly, stepping back from me out of respect.

"Yeah, well, but I…" stammering, I heard the leash clipping to my collar. I found myself leaving the poodle party without time to explain that I really didn't go into deep water at all. I just pounced on my ball, dug holes in the sand, and ran along the shallow sandy puddles with other pups. Flying was not something I did at Dog Beach.

Oh well, maybe the other pups didn't need to know everything about my new life anyway. I left the Bay Park happy and proud, my fluffy tail straight up, prancing poodle – style.

Water WILD!

One day at Dog Beach, My Lady called to me as she walked slowly from the shore into low waves. As she got in waist deep, she pushed a large amount of water in front of her, cupping and opening her hands as she raised them high, letting the water slide fast away. Hitting a small wave broadside with her forearm, she sent a tall wall of it splashing from her while walking away from me. The water was her toy.

"Hey!" I barked, "…don't leave!" I ran to the edge of the incoming tide. "What are you doing with that, that water? Let's play with the ball!" I yelped between my teeth holding the ball tightly as I pranced up and down the sand.

Turning to me briefly and smiling she moved slowly, throwing water on her face, "Prince, Prince Pounce-a-Lot, come on baby boy," she called over the crash of the small waves hitting the beach.

"Wait! Hey Lady, wait!" Tightening my grip on the ball in my mouth, I plunged in wildly to get to her, and suddenly, the water seeped through my sun - warmed fur, right to my skin. Cool and soothing as it was unexpected, I felt the water lift much of my weight. I was surprised at how easy it was to splash and move around in that wet stuff!

"Wow! Nice!" I jumped around in shoulder deep water, making my own white water bubbles. Splashing madly, suddenly I could see a good size wave moving slowly towards me. I visualized Ranger flying on it. Maybe I could do the same thing. Why not? Being in a good position to find out, I let the rising water come to me. The heap of water lifted my legs to dangle above the sea's sand bottom. And it felt like flying as I moved toward shore with the wave. I gently touched down to solid sand again. Wow!

From that day on, I galloped straight into the ocean to play with dogs and to bounce around in circles spewing water in all directions. Racing madly along the shallow incoming tidewater, my shiny wet fur flashing in the sun, I raced against time itself, as fast as any puppy had ever run or would ever run. I ran like a wild dog, chasing dogs and being chased. I ran so close between people talking to each other they stepped back as I shared water from my fur with their trousers. And I flew on waves!

Playing chase at Dog Beach, Del Mar

Coronado Dog Beach

Dog Beach, Carmel

Growing Up

As I grew, my long-legged proportions made me able to bounce and prance along as my normal way of walking. Everyone noticed me. Lori and I walked quickly through town because as she used to say, "We can't slow down and stop for everyone to pet you, my baby boy. We have places to go and things to do."

Many people and most children wanted to touch my bouncing curls as I pranced along the sidewalk.

When someone did approach and ask to pet me she would say, "Go slow and scratch softly under his chin. That's how his Mom used to tell him that she loved him. Then you can pet his head." She told them well, because even to this day if someone unfamiliar suddenly tries to touch the top of my head, I sometimes get frightened and try to run away.

My Fourth of July friend

Importantly, on our play dates, Dolly noticed and approved of my long legs and changing body. I outweighed her on my first birthday, and she had a hard time telling me what to do after that. Anyway, she didn't seem to want to be in charge of how we played all the time anymore. I still let her win most of our furious tug of wars over toys and I always let her catch the balls thrown for us. My Dolly and me! The way it had to be!

When Lori and Dolly's Mom have to work or attend activities where doggies are not invited, Dolly and I often attended the same dog sitting place. Sometimes we were there at the same day! It was a big air conditioned room with many toys. Dogs and pups ran freely and played all day. We each had our favorite playmates and toys there. Then, when Dolly decided play time was over, I sat or stood between her and all the other dogs. I even pushed dogs away from her. She was my Dolly and I was her Prince.

Training Anyone?

My Lady took me with her sometimes to her church and Bible study. One day we went with a church group to sing with older people who lived at a building by the Bay Park. Everyone made such a fuss over me! Many ladies and a few nice gentlemen petted me gently. They all were in agreement when one of them said, "Come again! We would love to see Prince anytime."

Right then, I think, Lori got the idea that she and I could be good at volunteering to visit people in care centers and hospitals. She liked talking to people and I was fun, good natured, and fluffy.

My obedience training started right then, well, sort - of started. Every day after that at home she began to tell me to sit, stay, lie down, and come to her. Then she gave me treats if I did what she said.

I thought to myself, "Hey, this is boring, let's mix it up a bit!"

Lori would tell me, "Down." Sometimes I would lie down immediately and neatly in front of her. My front feet would be together with all my toes in perfect alignment. Other times, I would twirl a few times in a circle and end up lying down with my back to her. She then had to walk around in front of me, telling me more things to do. But by making her walk around me, I was also telling her what to do! Then, sometimes, instead of lying down, I would leap up quickly to lick her face. I let her know that all this talk about "down" was not too much fun.

We both laughed a lot during these first training sessions. She decided I was too young and fun loving for obedience training. But if we had continued training when I was very young it would have gone a lot faster and would have been much easier for both of us. Believe me!

I was as selfish and independent as I was fun-loving. I pulled my leash hard. I stretched it out just a bit more than I thought possible to meet and dance with every passing dog. I pulled on it to reach every puddle of rain water in my path. Why didn't Lori just let that leash go? I remained the "leader" between us about half the time. That was fair, right? We were two, so it seemed right to split the leadership responsibility. My mom Britte had probably underestimated my leadership ability. I thought I was very good at being Top Dog. I was the one who made our outings interesting by changing direction every few seconds, as I pranced as close to my top speed as I could encourage Lori to follow.

After a long time running and splashing at Dog Beach, she would finally call me to come to her so we could leave. Demanding more play time, I usually pivoted wildly in circles and then pushed with my back legs to blast off like a little rocket. Running away, I soon looked like a small dot on the horizon to her. I would only let her catch me as I fell to the ground exhausted, panting and rolling over, feet in the air and smiling to make her laugh.

I soon grew large and strong enough to pull Lori off balance. She began to raise her voice unpleasantly to me, and that was hard on both of us. One day my pulling caused her great distress. She hurt her hand and fell to the ground. I wagged my tail and head, bowing to her to join me in playing again and licked her hurting hand. I decided it was not fun to hurt My Lady Lori.

Around that time, I believe, Lori found that the two of us could become a "Volunteer Pet Therapy Team" at a local hospital, if only I would obey her.

I could feel and almost hear Lori's frustration. I did hear her say out loud, to a friend, that if I obeyed her in front of a qualified Dog Trainer (Passing a test for <u>Canine Good Citizenship</u> certified by the <u>American Kennel Club</u>) and passed the same test in front of people at a local hospital in La Jolla, it would mean that she and I would receive volunteer "Pet Therapy Team" badges that would allow us to visit patients and hospital staff on a regular basis.

Now she was getting serious about telling me what to do. I took it all as good fun, and kept joking around with her. I only obeyed a few times in a row. Then I would ask her to dance with me, or trot away to find something interesting to do besides the same boring drill. And I continued to pull hard on the leash.

At some point near my eighth month, Lori hired a professional dog training company. The trainers treated me like a bad dog. They trained us in a group of dogs with their people.

One of them, a short stout woman, had red hair split into stubby pigtails sticking straight out behind her ears. She took my leash to show Lori how to make me do things. "Hey!" I yelped on my first day, turning my head back to My Lady at every jerk of my neck and voice command to heel to the trainer's side, "Hey this is hurting me! Do you care? How can you allow this neck jerking? I am Top Dog sometimes after all! Ouch! I mean, I am your sweet Prince Pounce-a-Lot, right?"

Lori learned to snap the leash hard like they did to make me heel to her side. Then I got further snaps until I walked with a loose leash, not pulling at all. I learned, but it was not fun. Their command voice was not sweet either! And they made Lori talk like they did.

Lori probably thought there may be a better way than such rough treatment. However, because I was a big poodle, she needed me to obey her. We continued the weekly lessons. I sulked, tail between my legs the whole hour each week. I tried to leave the lessons by slowly wandering, right up to the end of the leash, anyway. Hoping to disappear, I would lean against nearby walls pretending I was deaf, protesting all commands. I hoped to just fold myself up into the smallest ball of disappointed fur on the planet.

Dolly's Good Advice

I told Dolly my training troubles during one of our play dates at her house. "I can't stand it. Those trainers jerk my neck so that it hurts all night! And they speak meanly to me, making me almost believe I am a bad dog, even when I am doing what they want me to do." I sank my head low, "They just want me to walk without pulling on the leash, just behind them or at their side. It is all so boring.

At least Lori lets me do what I want sometimes."

"Look, my sweet Prince-ling you will come to understand someday that you are, in fact, not Top Dog, and that it is all OK, you will be fine," Dolly spoke in soothing tones.

"Well," I went on, "they don't understand that it would be much better for all of us, and a lot more fun to follow what I do, exploring everything, not just walking in circles over and over and so slow, slow – slow. Don't they know I am a much better Top Dog than they could ever try to be? But they don't even give me a chance."

"These trainers are in your life only for a short time." Dolly said. "They are teaching your Lady how to tell you to do what she wants you to do. It is all about saving her time. Your Lady pleases you as much as she can from what you say about your walks and beach runs. Remember how she helped you enjoy the waves? Make her happy, and then you will BOTH be happy!"

We wrestled for a while, trying to get control of a ball. Then Dolly pulled one of her stuffed toys from the overflowing toy chest in the living room. She plopped it directly in front of me as I flopped down to completely cover her old puppy bed.

Looking with pleasure at the toy, I whispered, "Who wants to listen to those harsh tones coming from those mean trainers? There is no music in their voices."

"Well, that doesn't sound like much fun," Dolly said. "I can't believe your Lady doesn't quit them. I was trained with sweet talk and plenty of treats, and that worked for me!"

As I listened to her, I stretched my neck to reach her generously presented toy. I took it into my mouth and my playful Dolly grabbed it at the same time. She held it fast at the other end, standing. We looked at each other over the soft toy, trying not to laugh. Slowly, I tugged it towards me, pulling her head to bow down. She then slowly pulled up her head, making my chin rise. Each of us held on tightly, pulling and then releasing our pull on that stuffed toy over and over in a slow motion sharing instead of our usual rowdy tug – of – war play.

Suddenly Dolly let it go to me and laid down with her front legs surrounding my head and shoulders.

"Oh my Prince!" She sighed softly putting her muzzle alongside mine as I held the prize she gave me. Quickly flipping on my back, I let that toy fly off wherever it wanted to go and touched her warm chin with my nose. My Dolly had finally called me by my real name! I was her Prince.

I stayed in her embrace a long time. Our play dates never came soon enough.

Passing the Test!

Soon after that My Lady quit our weekly training – torture lessons. We drilled the commands on our own. She used a strong voice, but not in a rough way. We still went to the mean training place, but only on test days to try to pass the Canine Good Citizenship test.

On test days, I always joked around. I flipped on my back when I was to heel and walk quietly by her side. I walked between the cones I was supposed to walk alongside. I did almost everything in a creative fun way. Lori was nervous on test days, so I became her joking dog to help her laugh and relax.

She did laugh, even on test days, but My Lady Lori was not happy. "Oh Prince, baby, my Beebe...how will anyone in the hospital know you are such a sweet dog if they can't meet you? Why won't you be serious about passing your test?" My lady would call me pet names and sigh in disappointment.

I guess she was going to give up on her plans for our Pet Therapy Team volunteer work. But then she heard about another instructor's training method of giving treats and praise instead of harsh commands.

My new trainer rewarded me with treats, praise, and petting for doing things upon her command. The neck jerks and harsh command voice were replaced only by ignoring me. Me ignored? No way! I got the idea and obeyed in that first training session. I PASSED the test the next time we came for class! I became an official American Kennel Club "Canine Good Citizen"!

Shaina Clapper, Trainer: www.AKC.org

Playing at Del Mar Dog Beach

Dog Beach, Del Mar

Learning the Ropes as a Hospital Pet Therapy Team

We received our certificate for passing the test after a couple of weeks. Then, along with several other sweet dogs, we passed our final set of command tests at the hospital. At last we were ready to volunteer to visit people in the hospital.

Coordinator of a local Hospital Pet Therapy Program

On our first day of volunteer visiting, we tagged behind a veteran volunteer Pet Therapy team. The older dog slowed his pace as we entered the first patient room. Turning to me he said, "Just lower your energy level kid. Keep your pretty prancing for the public hallways. Most people like to watch you bounce, but the people out there in the halls are not as bad off as the ones in these rooms. People in here are getting better from big hurts and problems with their bodies. They are tired most of the time. It is our job to give them a break in their day, to remind them that there are things beyond this room that they will be going back to soon enough. Things like beautiful animals, people to talk to and whatever they remember as being good."

I didn't have time to respond to the dog as he gently set his head on a bed near a feeble hand. He let that stranger slowly touch his head! That was interesting because he did not even know the man! The stranger in the bed laughed a deep happy laugh, "Good....dog...good..." his voice trailed off softly, and then pulling his hand from the dog, he managed a "...thank...you..." The veteran volunteer dog quickly pulled himself away from the bed and we all marched out. "Kid, when they say "THANK YOU", it is your signal to leave the room, ok?"

The dog trotted with energy down the hall and we all followed. Catching up to him as he slowed to enter another room, I asked "But what if they don't get better?"

"Son, most of them do get better, and now you are part of the team to encourage them on their journey home. Now just go to each one of them, and remind them that they are cared about. Give them a chance to communicate, to say something in words or just by touching you. That's all."

I pondered his words and learned many things that day.

Our Volunteer Work as a Pet Therapy Team

Lobby visitors and hospital staff loved to pet me on my regular volunteer rounds. Most of the doctors and nurses had serious jobs. When I came around for a visit they relaxed for a little while. Several of them had treats waiting for me when I arrived.

Staff Doctor

I wagged my tail and put my fluffy head near their hands. If I felt that they had strong fingernails, I put them to work by slowly turning to present my hind legs for some good deep scratching.

The veteran dog who trained me that first day was right about the lower life energy of the people in the rooms. They seemed to be like the older people living together in the residence by the Bay Park that Lori and I had visited long ago. However, many people in the hospital were quite young. They had gotten into accidents or had some kind of hidden problems inside their bodies that slowed them down. Most were happy to have a fluffy visitor. Others were too tired or too sick to visit.

Sometimes we came and went in and out of rooms quickly hearing a "thank you". Other times younger people could and would talk and laugh a long time. Conversations about dogs went on so long I would take the opportunity to lie down on the cool floor, becoming a breathing rug in the room.

My friend at church

30

During our first few weeks at volunteering, a tall man sitting quietly next to his bed motioned wordlessly for me to come near. His arms fell soft around my shoulders as he wept violently. He had lost his best hunting buddy, his golden retriever, a couple weeks before our visit. Now he was busy healing from surgery on his heart. As he sobbed, he shared with us some happy memories of his dog. Lori began to cry with him. I stood quiet in front of him as long as he wanted to caress me. I felt grief come out of him while his touch soothed me. I learned it is very good medicine for people and dogs to have company when they cry. Sometimes only a few words or gestures of encouragement are needed in this type of sharing towards healing.

About four months ago I approached a room and Lori knocked on its half open door. "Therapy dog today?"

"Come in please," a nice woman in the bed spoke softly, "but we have our own therapy dog today!" A man sitting across the room chuckled as the woman moved her feet under the small brown and white doggie on her bed. Her doctor had written a prescription for her dog to visit! We enjoyed talking, and learned something new again. A prescription for a dog visit! Nice!

These days as we walk by patient rooms, I pull Lori away from or towards certain doors. Where I pull her to visit, she knocks and asks the people inside if we can enter and we are always very welcome. When I pull her away from doors, and if she still wants to go in, I just stop moving. She has to give me a small tug to enter. People in these rooms when asked don't usually want to see a Pet Therapy Team anyway.

Staff Nurse

Staff Nurses

She says it is a wonder how I know who wants to see me as we are passing by. I always just know who would like a visit and who would not, and not always by smell or sound. I just know. And I wonder how she doesn't know. I get the feeling she thinks I am smarter than she is about many things. Maybe so, but I'd rather say that we make a great team!

On a recent visit, two patients enjoyed our visit so much that they asked Lori for information on taking the hospital test so they can visit people with their dogs too. This is good, because it means they are thinking of a good future. And it will be good to have more Volunteer Pet Therapy teams!

Hospital Yappy Hour with Volunteer Pet Therapy Teams, 2015

Hound Dog Instinct

I invite My Lady Lori into my world too, all the time! She enjoys the timeless relaxing way we play together. A two - year old prancing poodle, I now bounce by Lori's side, matching the speed she wants to walk, not pulling or running wildly. Our many hours together have trained me to do mostly what she asks me to do. After our play time or walks she seems refreshed and ready to take on her own world again.

But why can't I train her instead of her training me all the time? Our car is heading out to Dog Beach early this morning. We may arrive in time to find at least a few morning birds feeding along the water's edge. I hope to train Lori to 'Bird-Dog' with me. Sharing my hunting instinct with her will be exciting. I hope she is not as disobedient as I was as a pup. We will see.

Here we are, at Dog Beach. Good-bye leash! The smell of kelp invites me to breathe deeply as we push dry sand behind our feet. Ok, here we are at the ocean's edge. Let me just flatten myself down low and creep toward that flock of birds walking through the outgoing tide water. Oh good! Most of them split off walking fast or flying inland. I look to find Lori. Why is she walking? She is my partner and needs to be standing in one place so I can direct a bird to her. Oh well, it is 'Bird-Dogging' practice for her too, I guess. "Lori, stay!" I say by turning and staring at her briefly. She stops. Good. I lower myself to creep again. I hear her walking and need to look back at her again. "Lori, STAY!" I say by standing up tall and glaring at her. Good. She is stopped in her tracks. Now, I crouch down again and move slowly.

Ok, one bird is turning to look at me while the others fly off. That one bird is in perfect position. I creep slowly away from the water and slightly away from the bird, like I am going to walk away from the ocean. The bird relaxes and continues to walk slowly - toward Lori! I circle back to it. Good! It is walking faster now - how perfect!

I allow the bird to walk faster than I do, to let it think it can put distance between us without flying. NOW! I leap high and POUNCE with mighty force in the water just behind the bird. With no time to squawk or turn to the side, the bird takes off flying directly in front of Lori. "Good dog." I tell myself.

Now I take a moment to trot up to Lori and get my praise. She has seen something amazing. She pets me and talks proudly to me. I am not leaving her side until she puts on my leash and then lets me go again. This little leashing ceremony finishes the job in my mind.

Ok, I'm off leash again. Now, let's see, where did that bird land? He's up the beach a ways, near the houses. So let me creep, creep, now pounce! The bird is flying right in front of Lori again!

Well, this time was easier for me. Even jumping in sand without the added splash of water, I could aim my bird-dog pouncing to make the bird fly over Lori more directly, because she stood in one place watching me. Now let me get hooked to that leash again, and receive her praise. With my leadership, we have done some very successful 'Bird - Dogging'. If Lori were a hunter, we probably would have caught the bird together.

Not many people are like my Lori. She took my directions and allowed herself to receive training from me, her dog. I am proud and happy that she listened to me. She probably feels the same way about me when I do what she tells me to do. Mutual cooperation can really makes us a good team.

After I take my time playing with other pups in the water, and get in some fancy body surfing on top of a few waves, Lori calls me to come to her. I run to her side. Her happiness in my quick response becomes our mutual happiness. And I can teach her more games another day. For now, I will respond to her and obey, most of the time!

It will be time for a big snooze when I get home. I hope my next play date with

Dolly comes soon. I know she will love to hear about my 'Lori training day' at the beach. Here we are, in the door and to bed!

David and Prince

The End

Post script

So that is our story, according to my Prince. But there is more. Perhaps out of politeness towards me or modesty he finds it difficult to speak about how he has changed me. Or perhaps giving is just so much a part of the dog in him that he takes his transforming effect on me as no big deal. I will attempt to unfold some of the dynamics of a dog–human partnership now, supported by recent scientific study. While I am not sure of the real value to him of things he has learned or gained from our relationship together, I know he has extended the horizon of my own emotional intelligence and I am a better person for knowing him.

DOG BEACH:

A public place at the ocean's edge where dogs and humans can run and swim freely without leashes.

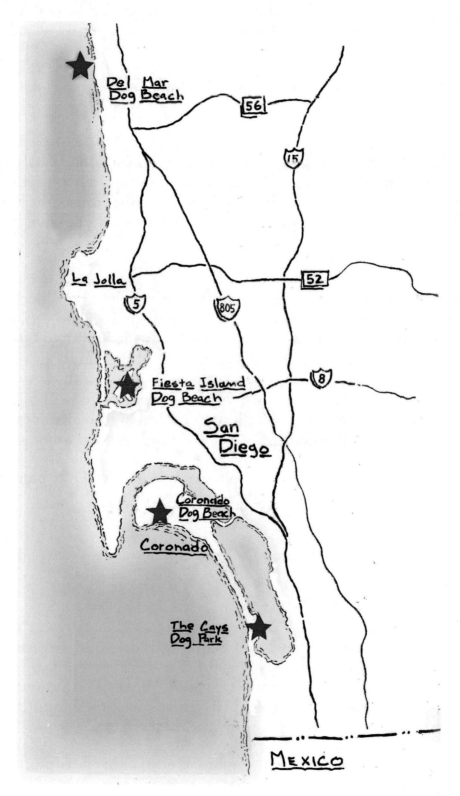

DOG BREEDER:

A good breeder studies the pedigrees and attributes of generations of dogs before ever making a breeding decision. Such dedication is not immediately apparent the day a litter of puppies is born. But all that unseen work pays enormous dividends down the road when the puppies turn into beautiful adults with correct temperament and structure. -Sheila Goffe, Director, AKC

Prince was bred at: www.bpoodles.com in Encinitas, CA

DOG PACK:

Feral dogs form "packs" consisting of three or four boded male/female pairs. The dogs usually mate for life, but are not always monogamous when having pups. As raising pups is time consuming and difficult for one dog, the male of the bonded pair will help his mate raises her pups, even if they are not his own biological offspring.

(I believe Dolly and Prince are mated for life).

While research is inconclusive about whether or not dogs consider humans as dog pack members, it is obvious to me that dominance of the person is to be established over the dog to have a good relationship and ability to co-exist with each other and exist well in the world. Otherwise, a dominant dog will try to let everyone, including their humans, know when to play, when the people can and cannot leave them. This may be because dog pack behavior allows leaders to leave the pack, but the followers are not to leave. A dominant dog can act out when what are considered the followers leave, chewing and ruining household things.

"Dog Behavior" Wikipedia: https://en.wikipedia.org/wiki/Dog_behavior

"Monogamy and polygyny in canids" October 20, 2012 by Retrieverman

see more: http://retrieverman.net/2012/10/20/monogamy-and-polygyny-in-canids/

DOG TRAINING:

Dog training is a great way to bond with your dog and to learn how to communicate with your dog. There are many forms of dog training. The form of dog training I used with Prince was positive reinforcement. Positive reinforcement is reward-based training. This means when Prince did something I liked, I gave him attention for it by means of praise, treats and playtime.

-Shaina Clapper, dog Trainer and Canine Good Citizen Evaluator for the American Kennel Club www.AKC.org

DOG'S EYES: EMOTIONAL INTELLIGENCE BY READING THE RIGHT EYE

Dogs are the only animals that can read emotion in faces much like humans, cementing their position as man's best friend, claim scientists.

"Dogs can read emotion in human faces"

By Richard Alleyne, Science Correspondent for The Telegraph October 29, 2008

See more of the article:

http://www.telegraph.co.uk/news/science/science-news/3354028/Dogs-can-read-emotion-in-human-faces.html

DOG'S EYES: ANXIETY REDUCTION BY LOOKING INTO THE EYES OF A DOG

Japanese researchers found that dogs who trained a long gaze on their owners had elevated levels of oxytocin, a hormone produced in the brain that is associated with nurturing and attachment, similar to the feel-good feedback that bolsters bonding between parent and child. After receiving those long gazes, the owners' levels of oxytocin increased, too.

The dog's gaze cues connection and response in the owner, who will reward the dog by gazing, talking and touching…which helps solder the two, the researchers said.

"The Look of Love Is in the Dog's Eyes" Well Pets, (a New York Times blog)

By Jan Hoffman April 16, 2015

See more of the articles:

http://well.blogs.nytimes.com/2015/04/16/the-look-of-love-is-in-the-dogs-eyes

http://www.sciencemag.org/content/348/6232/333)

DOGS DETECT DISEASE

Researchers in Germany followed a program developed at the Cleveland Clinic that trained dogs to detect the smell of a waste product of lung cancer.

Dogs also can be trained to detect … the onset of high blood pressure, a heart attack and epileptic seizures, and to get a person the help he or she needs.

How dogs detect cancer, other diseases in humans with smell: Drs. Oz and Roizen June 11, 2012

http://www.cleveland.com/healthfit/index.ssf/2012/06/how_dogs_detect_cancer_other_d.ht

PET THERAPY ANIMALS

Pet therapy is a guided interaction between an individual and a trained animal. It also involves the animal's handler. The purpose of pet therapy is to help a patient recover from or cope with a health problem or a mental disorder. Pet therapy also is called animal-assisted therapy (AAT).

Dogs and cats are the animals most commonly used in pet therapy. However, fish, guinea pigs, horses, and other animals that meet screening criteria can be used. The type of animal chosen depends on the therapeutic goals of a patient's treatment plan.

Healthline Web site: http://www.healthline.com/health/pet-therapy#Overview1

Hospital Staff

SERVICE DOGS

Prince is a Pet Therapy Volunteer dog, not a Service Dog.

Here is the definition of "Service Animal" from the Americans with Disabilities Act:

"Service animals are defined as dogs that are individually trained to do work or perform tasks for people with disabilities.

Examples of such work or tasks include guiding people who are blind, alerting people who are deaf, pulling a wheelchair, alerting and protecting a person who is having a seizure, reminding a person with mental illness to take prescribed medications, calming a person with Post Traumatic Stress Disorder (PTSD) during an anxiety attack, or performing other duties. Service animals are working animals, not pets. The work or task a dog has been trained to provide must be directly related to the person's disability. Dogs whose sole function is to provide comfort or emotional support do not qualify as service animals under the ADA."

A service dog can learn many tasks to assist the owner who might be experiencing sudden flare up symptoms, side effects of medications, or be in a situation in which outside help is needed.

List of tasks

- Bringing medication to alleviate symptoms
- Medication reminder at a certain time of day
- Bring a beverage so the patient can swallow the medication
- Bring the emergency phone during a crisis
- Provide balance assistance on stairs
- Assist person to rise and steady themselves
- Respond to smoke alarm if partner is unresponsive
- Backpacking medical related supplies or information
- Provide tactile stimulation to disrupt an emotional overload
- Wake up human partner for work or school
- Lighting up dark rooms
- Keep suspicious strangers away

September 15, 2010, the United States Department of Justice, Civil Rights Division, Disability Rights Section, issued "ADA 2010 Revised Requirements; Service Animals".

About the Author

Fay Lorraine Sueltz, AIA, CASI, ICC, practices Architecture in Southern California. She is also an architectural consultant regarding the Federal Americans with Disabilities Act and the California Building Code.

The emotional intelligence of her pet Standard Poodle, Prince, compelled her to write about his adventures and also theirs together as a volunteer Pet Therapy Team at Scripps Memorial Hospital, La Jolla, California.

Printed in the United States
By Bookmasters